T0195955

THE GOLDEN TREASURE BOOK

INSPIRATIONAL POEMS FOR MEDITATION
AND OPENING OF THE MIRROR MIND,
FOR MENTAL ILLUMINATION AND ENLIGHTENMENT

JOHN GENT AND GRETA DABEK

authorHOUSE®

AuthorHouse™ UK
1663 Liberty Drive
Bloomington, IN 47403 USA
www.authorhouse.co.uk
Phone: 0800.197.4150

Published by AuthorHouse 04/05/2019

ISBN: 978-1-7283-8261-6 (sc)
ISBN: 978-1-7283-8527-3 (e)

THE GOLDEN TREASURE BOOK

INSPIRATIONAL POEMS FOR MEDITATION
AND OPENING OF THE MIRROR MIND,
FOR MENTAL ILLUMINATION AND ENLIGHTENMENT

THE SEEKER'S JOURNEY THROUGH
THE POWER CENTRES AND BARRIERS

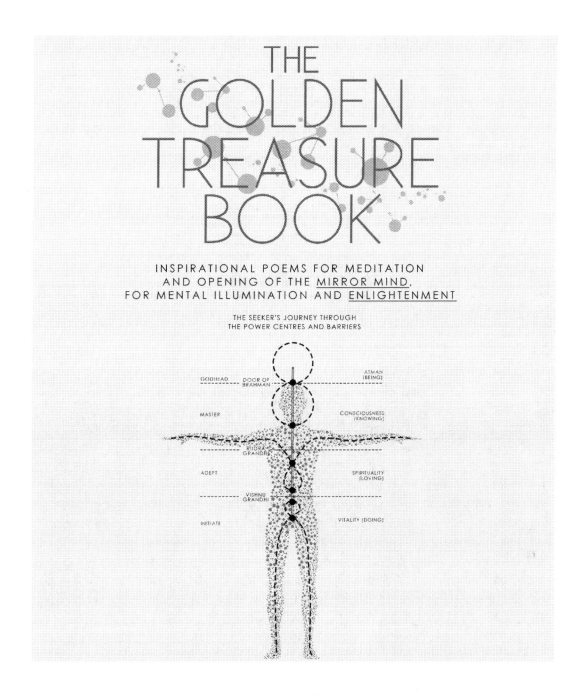

The consciousness of man is so dimly lit that it is impossible for him to see the reality which surrounds him. The quality of his mind is also in such poor condition that it constantly make mistakes illusion for truth. His awareness is like that of a candle in a large room with only that which is closest being lit and the rest seen at best only in silhouette and the rest in darkness.

Progress towards reality is made when the mind is polished into highly reflective mirror like surface which can be fashioned to focus the light of consciousness to pierce the darkness of the unknown. When this beam of light can be directed by **concentration** at the will of the seeker, it illuminates everything upon which it is directed with sparkling radiance and clarity. The trained mind can then **meditate** upon these brightly lit perceptions and begin to understand the reality which they represent. When this process of directed and concentrated awareness and Self understanding becomes integrated, the third and final stage of **samadhi** is achieved and the Inner Being and the outer reality become merged.

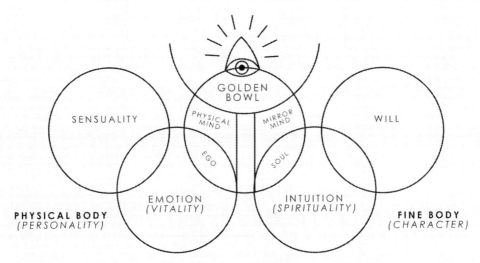

THE INSTRUMENTS OF CONSCIOUSNESS

THE CROSS ROADS OF DESTINY

Little children, their minds filled with wonder soon start trying to find out the truth about the strange and intriguing world in which they find themselves. They regularly consult the giants of this land, whom they regard as the established Gods. They constantly bombard them with questions and get all sorts of weird answers, which serves only to increase their puzzlement. Christmas comes around and that huge and benevolent old gentleman with thick red coat and bushy white beard stealthily delivers presents of the child's choice in the dead of the night. Amongst the fascinating toys, one inevitably finds a large book often called the Golden Treasure Book. This book is filled with pictures of dinosaurs, ancient cities and stars and planets. At least in this book the child must find out all that he wishes to know.

Twenty years later our little child is now himself an established God with little children of his own who ask the same eternal questions. Unfortunately, he has learned very little in all this time and the answers which he gives his children are the same inadequate ones which he received himself.

This is the lot of the average man, he never learns the real and basic truths of life, and after he reaches maturity he usually ceases trying. The dirty devices of adult humanity are by now much more intriguing to his mind.

SUBJECTS FOR MEDITATION

Introduction xi
How To Experience Tai-Chi 1
The Transformation Of Field Energy 2
Five Systems Of Thought 3
Way Of The Wanderer 4
The Inner Power 5
Wisdom Of King Tzu 6
The Middle Way 7
The Way Of Tai-Chi-Chuan 8
The Unspeakable Truth 9
Super Mind 10
Immortality 11
The Skilful Path 12
The Mysterious Power 13
Skilful Tai-Chi-Chuan 14
Karma 15
Order 16
Self Reliance 17
Perfection 18
Health 19
The Self 20
The Inner Light 21
Secrets 22
Wonder 23
The Gateway 24
Illumination 25
Awakening 26
Ming 27
The Universe Within 28
Powers 29
Forces 30
Gaia 31
Reality 32
Tao 33
Chi-Kung 34
The Sage 35
Enlightenment 36
The Witness 37
The Inner Will 38
Sung 39

INNER STILLNESS
By
John Gent and Greta Dabek.

When I do not disturb the non action of my inner peace,
I receive gentle wisdom and guidance from within.
This serene emptiness rests in me as I sleep
And stills my awareness during the busy working days.
It feeds my mind with pleasant reassuring thoughts
And I know I am safe from the troubles of the world.

I feel happy when I do not resist the stillness within me,
As my feelings relax to allow it to calm my weary body.
My mind glows with crystal purity and the surface of my flesh
Radiates the golden glow of happiness and perfect health.
In order that this transient body can become a worthy temple
I must keep it pure for the perfection of the Inner Being.

Written and published
in 2002 by John Gent,
17, Little Carter Lane,
Mansfield, Notts. NG18 3AA
England, UK

John Gent was taught yoga at eight years old. He became a yoga teacher in 1948. He formed several yoga organisations in England in the 1960s. Since then, he has written books from 1968 to present day on numerous aspects of yoga including Chinese Taoist, Indian, Tibetan and Egyptian. He has written many books that have reached different parts of the world.

Greta Dabek has studied John Gent's teaching for the last ten years and is a yoga teacher. She is now a co-author of this poetry book that has been revised with John Gent.

INTRODUCTION

By

John Gent and Greta Dabek.

This book of poems is designed as a study for those who are interested in exploring the mysteries of yoga. The concise rhythmic patterns of poetic verse are ideally suited for conveying difficult psychological and philosophical truths in a direct easy to understand manner. In many ways, it is superior to the complex detail involved when the same material is explained using the dull fabric of ordinary prose.

These poems cover many of the mystical secrets of the masters especially some of the deeper aspects involving direct non-dual experience of reality as it is and the teaching dates back to ancient times. With the fighting and turmoil all over the Orient in recent times, most of the old monastic systems are now in serious decline. As a result, the gems preserved in this book may one day become valuable again.

The format of these poems involves five verses or stanzas, respectively, and we have found this system an ideal way of conveying what we have to say. The first verse introduces the subject and the second longer verse, enlarges on it. The third and fourth verses add detail and the last one offers a conclusion. These poems make ideal material for study and meditation and can be used in conjunction with formal training by those making progress in yoga practice.

HOW TO EXPERIENCE TAI-CHI
By
John Gent and Greta Dabek.

When the Tao acts through our mind without hindrance
Then we will harm no one by our thoughts and actions
And feel ourselves to be neither gentle or kind
As we know not where we go but neither are we lost.
We seek no personal goal but do not despise those who do.

When we allow the Tao to operate in us without resistance
We cease to struggle to attain fame and fortune in the world
And neither do we make a virtue of poverty and austerity.
Then we experience the joy of having nothing to defend
As we place no value upon our possessions and position in life.
We rely not on others and feel no pride when we walk alone.
We no longer need company but do not condemn those who do.

When we allow the Tao to work in us without interference,
Reward loses its appeal and disgrace and shame does not deter us.
Tao remains unknown even though we feel its presence within.
As we travel our path through the triumphs and disasters of life
Virtue produces nothing and as we forget ourselves in the Tao,
We discover the importance of an empty mind that cools passion.

When Tao flows through us without restriction and restraint,
We become simple in our needs and spontaneous in our deeds.
Its presence within us takes responsibility for all our actions
Neither endorsing or defending them and in this freedom
There is nothing to which we have to conform or believe.
By losing our way, we experience a delight we cannot comprehend.

When Tao merges with the very heart of our being,
All our actions dissolve into one as we become stationary
And watch with interest the restless, moving events of life
Revolving in a whirlpool around our calm centre of stillness.
By non-action we will rest in the total security of the Tao.

THE TRANSFORMATION OF FIELD ENERGY
By
John Gent and Greta Dabek.

Field energy is the power that lies dormant in the human frame
And those who can activate its forces, hold the key to life.
Dark form is the preferred state of matter in our world
And as its power is frozen, we survive by working with our hands,
When our minds can unlock unlimited forces to supply our needs.

The power of the universe is invisible to mortal eyes of flesh
As we grovel and squabble our way through short primitive lives,
And inhale the precious nectar from the gods on every breath.
There behind our many thoughts dwell enormous powers of attention
Which can hear the sound of silence and know the secret of the calm.
Only those of quiet mind and contented heart can experience truth
As we open the inner eye to see beyond the illusion of time.

Those whose minds are unruffled and still, illuminate as a mirror
That reflects truth upon the empty screen of the awareness
And awakens the latent field energies asleep in the body.
Then we know their nature and can bring them into harmony
To balance the cooling fluids of the Earth with Heavenly power
And learn the secrets of yin and yang that transform the body.

The body is mortal only in its crystalised, mechanical form,
But those who can etherealise its atoms can extend its life.
When all its separate parts become one in a single energy field,
Then there is no part of it that can wear out or decay.
The mind that can hold all the forces together in their place,
Can also express the perfection of the spirit that operates it.

The unenlightened soul moves in endless bodily incarnations,
On a conveyor belt of lost opportunity, suffering and pain.
By transforming just one of these many bodies through virtue,
We can illuminate each atom with divine power and be free
From the death of form and ride the subtle forces of freedom.

FIVE SYSTEMS OF THOUGHT
By
John Gent and Greta Dabek.

When we objectify the mind and use it as an instrument for study
Of the living world that is external and within the awareness,
We cease to be engrossed in our personal lives and can explore
The five systems of the mind by which our knowledge is attained
And thereby we begin to remember who we are and why we came here.

Subliminal thinking occurs as we hover on the threshold of sleep
And we observe our dreams and relive the happiness and horrors
Of life through our memories and thus see the error of our ways.
Our rational mind can be organised and controlled for the study
And evaluation of any subject, to solve problems and build ideas.
This dualist meditation involves language and picture thought
Projected on the screen of awareness to use as a guide to life.

Lateral thinking is an undisciplined, free-ranging form of thought
That frees the mind from the straight jacket of logic and reason.
The oriental sages encourage illogical meditation in which our
Irrational ideas, irrelevant to the subject, can solve problems.
Taoist thinking lets the beauty and cunning of the artistic mind
Calm the cruel logic of the world with the humanity of virtue.

Intuitive meditation is like the dream reflections of sublimation
But at the other extreme of the range in our personal awareness.
Just as reflective reverie unlocks information from our memories,
So intuitive thinking examines creative ideas from the intellect.
In this hyper alertness, we allow impressions to enter our minds
From the void and glimpse the joy of reality we cannot understand.

Visionary deliberation takes place when we lose our individuality
And contemplative awareness outshines our mundane ego personality.
In this supreme state of spiritual tai-chi we take no interest
In our personal survival and experience joy we cannot share.
Anyone can visit this realm of bliss and return to ordinary life.

WAY OF THE WANDERER
By
John Gent and Greta Dabek.

He who knows how to live can travel safely in the wilderness
As he avoids wild beasts and prevents use of tooth and claw.
He melts into the background and has nothing for thieves to steal.
By strength and humility he presents no threat to friend or foe.
He is successful and invulnerable and does not invite trouble.

The wanderer sees the danger beneath the surface of still water
And instinctively knows where his strengths and weaknesses lie.
His example invites others to follow his path and seek counsel.
By forgetting selfishness and becoming empty, he builds character
And undoing the bonds of pride and prejudice he finds humility.
He moves along the way of personal denial and impoverishment
And with this shedding of care, he is filled with freedom of the clouds.

Squandering our energies and dividing our strength invites ruin
But yielding with relaxed confidence before the rising tempest,
Holds together our inner power to protect us from the storm.
And when stillness prevails, we can emerge from our shelter
To rebuild and feel no sadness for the things we have lost.
Then our hearts fill with joy as the spirit rests in pure Being.

He who travels without guidance in a far land, will lose his way
And those who go beyond their depth without safety invite trouble.
To the empty wanderer, success and failure give equal experience
In a trackless road to the void in which a wrong turning may lead
To a quicker route but climbing too high can lead to a fall.
So be of good cheer and follow the middle way to perfection.

Great is the ingenuity of the creative mind from which all things
Are born to the many varied life forms on our populous planet.
The Sun shines, the clouds gather and the rain propagates the land
This allows the flora and fauna to thrive in their selected roles
In harmony with the eternal Presence that pervades all things.

THE INNER POWER
By
John Gent and Greta Dabek.

Field energy arises in the human body by the exercise of virtue
As it flows in the channels, building the radiant power of love
In the world by projecting inspired compassion and works of mercy
But these healing properties are stifled by the discord of anger
And its power is unknown when we spend our lives in selfishness.

Happiness comes to those who do not resist the stillness within.
As feelings relax into the serene calmness of the body and mind
To allow invisible energy to function in balance and harmony
So that the awareness shines with a dazzling, crystal clarity
And the body radiates the golden glow of fitness and health,
In order to make this fragile organism a pure and worthy temple
For the perfection of the divine Being who dwells within.

The exercise of non action does not disturb the inner peace
Which spreads its gentle guidance to the mind from within
And this tranquil stillness rests with us as we quietly sleep
To feed our dreams with many reassuring pictures and thoughts
That comforts the awareness through the pain of the working day
And enables us to accept the trouble and violence of the world.

Silence and stillness relax the actions of the body and mind
And allows the living spirit to light up the awareness
Without hindrance to fill the awareness with its peace and wisdom
To enable us to endure the mundane boredom of drab daily life
And make room for the illuminated astonishment at the grandeur
Of our planetary home and the intelligence that created it.

When spirit takes over the divided power of our emotional life,
We no longer feel hatred and anger towards those who provoke us
As this harmonised love power, radiates outwards from the heart
Filling each living cell with the unifying force of virtue
And through our actions, inspires those around us with great joy.

WISDOM OF KING TZU
By
John Gent and Greta Dabek.

Those who comply without determination become servile
And thereby, caution without purpose turns to timidity.
However, courage without restraint becomes rebelliousness,
And honesty without humility quickly degenerates into rudeness.
Thus, yin harnesses strength and yang protects our weaknesses.

To distinguish between propriety and misconduct requires wisdom
As only those who are mindful can discriminate without confusion.
It is less selfish to give than to beg. Those who accept favour
Should do so with little demonstration and much gratitude.
It is more courageous to stand your ground without aggression,
But given the choice of life or death, those who choose to live,
Should temper their courage with wisdom and redeem themselves.

Those who build up their relationships but fail in obligation,
Soon allow discord to cloud over the powers of discrimination
And so must learn to live with bitter competition and rivalry.
However, the Sage never justifies his objectives with argument
And retains his purpose by not contending them with others.
Thereby in keeping his counsel, he continues to dwell in peace.

The perfect argument cannot be expressed through words,
Neither can divine love be discovered in our actions.
That which is perfectly honest is not absolutely incorruptible,
Neither is indestructible courage completely unyielding.
For the light that illuminates the mind, is not the Tao
And the truth that Is, will always remain unmanifest.

Speech that argues will always miss the target of truth
And love that has limits will always turn towards desire.
Absolute courage falls into wrath through foolhardiness.
When the circle of spirit fits into the square of form,
The riddle of life will dissolve and death will pass away.

THE MIDDLE WAY
By
John Gent and Greta Dabek.

Seekers who are illuminated by the spirit are empty of self will
And though their bodies become twisted in old age they keep whole.
This light shines for all to see yet there are but few who perceive it,
For he who knows the way, finds the all pervading power within
That does not show itself but is known by its resilient energy.

Only the Sage knows the deep compassion of the primal unity
That is invisible to mortal eyes but can be found everywhere.
He is not proud of the work he does and gives it freely to all.
He does not defend his position to invite the contention of others
By indicating the way to others; he never defines it in mere words.
In not boasting what he can do, he reserves the power to succeed
Without showing his hand and so not drawing attention to himself.

The ego shows off his abilities that are limited as a consequence.
His conceited knowledge and worldly wisdom restricts his harmony
And the straightjacket of his pious morality knows not kindness.
He uses the skills of hand and eye only for selfish personal gain
But all his cunning cannot prevent thieves claiming their share
To leave behind, the lasting treasures of selfless simplicity.

Those who live in the world of duality, must constantly decide
For better or worse, between good and evil, by right or wrong.
Those who balance their efforts on the middle way, see the light
And carry no such burdens; by finding this poised, in-between state,
Remain alert, untroubled and attentive, in clear, unpolarised mind
That knows at the end of the journey, light and darkness are one.

The pervading life force spans the way between Observer and goal
And although invisible, it is perfectly complete in its wholeness.
It depends on nothing and lights the way without sound and form.
It fills the awareness of the illuminated, who are empty of vanity,
And does not fail to show them eternity in their hour of need.

THE WAY OF TAI-CHI-CHUAN
By
John Gent and Greta Dabek

If you allow chi to flow through your body without ceasing
You will become sensitive to the changes between yin and yang.
This embrace of stillness will then be found in gentle motion
As harmonious movement reveals the power of the stationary Self
And fills the awareness with a new level of understanding.

All movement should begin from the power source at the waist
And from its epicentre below the navel arises spontaneous action.
In the quiet flow of chi, motion and stillness achieve harmony
As every movement is made with feeling and meaningful awareness.
Never abandon your attention from the waist as chi will arise
When the abdomen is light and free with the stimulation of ching.
Then energy will flow up the spine to illuminate the awareness.

When Tai-chi training makes the body both pliant and soft
And the head becomes suspended as if from a thread from above,
You will remain awake to every tension and discord below.
Whether the body bends and stretches, opens or closes,
Let the natural way of movement through stillness be your guide
Along the noble path, to harmonic balance between mind and body.

First seek understanding of the instructions of your teacher
And then apply his words to your every movement and observation.
In this way, his skill will be applied through your own expertise
As the way of Tai-chi unveils within your illuminated awareness.
When the mind remains awake and attentive, this will promote
Harmony of the body and gentleness, youth and health will prevail.

First hold the mind quiet and steady by focusing the attention
So that every muscle moves with relaxed, responsive harmony.
For it only takes a tiny effort to deflect a powerful force
And by upsetting the balance and composure of your opponent,
You can then yield and counter his attack in a single move.

THE UNSPEAKABLE TRUTH
By
John Gent and Greta Dabek.

Fukasetsu is the unspeakable truth at the heart of mysticism
That eludes every means of expression and dualistic understanding
And those who realise this dream in the light of illumination
Stand astonished and mute before a spectacle they cannot explain
To their eager adherents who ardently seek an active sign.

The enlightened no longer fix their attention on the sacred texts
That see only the finger of verbal truth pointing to the light
And are but a vague indication of the place where reality hides.
The symbolic sight of the Sun's cosmic vision is blinding
To the gaze of the human eyes but can be captured and contained
Within the golden bowl of our enlightened awareness, that is
Empty of words, silent in virtue and pure in compassion.

The open gaze of Bodhi Sages speaks the silence of emptiness
And their unspoken love comforts those who see truth in a smile
That confirms the words they want to hear as a vacant sign
To sustain their faith along a path they follow but cannot know
And leads to a light they are unable to see as their minds
Are still filled with thoughts which deny the love they seek.

Truth that has no boundaries cannot be confined in books
And neither can it be recited in mantras of the spoken word.
But those whose awareness is lit by fukasetu's invisible glow
Can see the point in each single verse of the true dharma
And know that it is everywhere. And there is nothing without it
For those who have ears, that see the truth in a blackbird's song.

Those who balance the love of truth in their heart and mind,
Know that Heaven and Earth are equally high and evenly low.
The mountains and the marshes share the same level plain,
As all dual forces, and forms merge joy and misery in to one
In the ecstatic bliss that transcends them all in nirvana.

SUPER MIND
By
John Gent and Greta Dabek

That which can be observed and yet remains unseen,
That which can be listened to and yet remains unheard,
That which can be grasped and yet cannot be touched,
Is not understood by the functioning mind and thereby
Has no part to play in the world of mental duality.

There is a vision that no light can make brighter
That dwells in an emptiness no shadow can make darker.
Because our thoughts cannot define - that unaffected by time,
And forms the essence of nothingness - that, is only observed
By: the imageless perception of the non-dual super mind.
When we meet it, we cannot see the perfection of its face
And when it departs, it leaves no trace in our awareness.

Illumination appears when we see the void in things.
By, purposely, focusing the awareness upon quiescence,
Our activities are motivated by non-acting passiveness.
When all around us moves in chaotic and restless confusion,
We remain mindful in a silent and orderly stillness
As we spread the invisible power of our love and harmony.

That which formed our busy and ever evolving world
Has not been changed by these miraculous creations.
This silent voice that guides us, and the invisible hand
That clears a path with the wisdom of the ancient masters,
Was in place before Earth was fashioned from the Heavens
And will take us along the path to the source of all light.

Silent, invisible, unchanging and standing as one,
Our nameless Creator waits within our very essence:
To illuminate our awareness with unspoken wisdom
And a loving harmony that is beyond all understanding; and
To dissolve our personal suffering, in eternal light.

IMMORTALITY
By
John Gent and Greta Dabek.

Those who follow the path of learning gain in experience
But those who seek the Tao strive to forget worldliness
And by doing less and less, they achieve more and more.
Finally, although nothing is done, nothing is left undone.
By not interfering, things around us take their course.

Wu-wei is action, free from intention, desire and motivation
In which the practitioner does not intervene in activities,
Thereby allowing things to unfold according to their nature.
When our actions are confined to what is natural and necessary,
We cease to be involved in the complexities of everyday life
And discover peace and tranquility in silent watchfulness
To gain wisdom by learning Who we are and from whence we came.

Internal order within is achieved by not acting without
And thereby we build a presence according to our station.
Then, those around us modify their actions with our position
And are able to improve themselves by respecting our example.
This simplicity allows things to travel their natural course
And by skillful noninterference, achieve much for little effort.

The desire to act, focuses our attention upon the world,
But when this craving passes, we return to natural simplicity.
Without seeking to alter things, however imperfect they seem,
We will then retain our serene tranquility and dwell in peace.
In this way, we learn by watching and holding unto ourselves,
Pass on what we have learned, leaving no trace of our presence.

The still, silent emptiness within us has never been born
But neither will that which is without form pass away.
Therefore, if we would learn the secret of immortality,
We should begin by renouncing our attachment to name and fame
And find peaceful anonymity of Being in the empty present.

THE SKILFUL PATH
By
John Gent and Greta Dabek.

The Atman is the skilful observer that dwells in our awareness
Who is unknown to those who are slaves to the actions of the body.
By selfless conduct however, the seeker offers every act
And the reward it brings as a sacrifice to the spirit within
And thereby frees himself from the entanglements of living.

Those who are of clear mind, gain merit through knowledge
And those who overflow with affection from a loving heart,
Learn to give it freely without expectation of reward.
However, by the very nature of the world in which we live,
We must all act to improve the life we share with others
And happily do the work necessity imposes upon us each day,
With cheerful unselfishness carrying the load others cannot bear.

All things arise from the spirit and are nourished by virtue.
Like everything else, we are fashioned like clay from matter
And are moulded into what we become by environmental change.
We, however, have the capacity to rise above our animal roots
By nurturing the tender skills of the spirit with selfless love,
And when the body passes away, it leaves behind the enduring Self.

When we learn the secret of living happily through love
And restrain our desires with the discipline of never too much,
We will shun pride by not seeking fame and attention of others
And thereby develop the skill of courage and taming our fears.
By not doing too much, we will always retain a reserve of power
As only love can destroy our enemies by turning them into friends.

The body is a mysterious temple in which there dwell two beings.
One is the self of the flesh and the other is of the soul.
If we follow the fortunes of the world and deny the spirit,
Our life will bring us mixed fortune, old age and death.
But by dwelling in the light of the soul, we have life eternal.

THE MYSTERIOUS POWER
By
John Gent and Greta Dabek.

Those who bring compassion and joy into the world anonymously
Can retain quiescence of mind and the rhythmic harmony within
And by focusing the power of the breath, spread healing power.
Love dispels our ignorant confusion to reveal the inner vision,
In our awareness, that allows us to see the hidden mysteries.

Those who wish to achieve union with the creative power within
Must become gentle and in this receptivity play the female role
To allow the mind to penetrate along fine channels in the way
That water permeates the lowest places and rises within forms.
Our awareness can go where the senses cannot to the secret places
Observing without interfering, to understand the mysteries
And knowing the part we are designed to play in the life to come.

The mysterious power in the body is greater than the flesh
And much larger than the sum total of its individual parts.
The attention of the untrained eye focuses only on the forms
That move and change in every conceivable way to excite the mind.
It is the space that contains nothing where the real power lies
And by becoming an empty vessel, we can hold the heavenly forces.

The riddle of life lies not in appearances but in the energy
That holds them together in their place to the single root
From whence they grew and when they have served their purpose
In created form, they return with their experience to begin
In another role, between the single essence and the many forms.
Female energies return to source and the male seeks expression.

The path leads the student from his conditioned existence
Within the human frame to an illumination in which is revealed
The purpose of our perceptive awareness with a new understanding
Of nature's subtle mysteries, too deep for the mind to comprehend.
But by knowing our inner Self, we also discover the secret of life.

SKILFUL TAI-CHI-CHUAN
By
John Gent and Greta Dabek.

When your opponent applies the pressure of aggressive power
You should yield and bend before the onslaught of his attack,
But if he should then seek his refuge in evasion and the retreat,
Then stick with him and work in harmony with his every move.
So that he cannot avoid you or find a space in which to hide.

Match the speed of your adversary by mirroring his every move
So that when he attempts surprise, he fails to catch you unaware.
Should he suddenly change to slowness and stealth, then follow.
Be patient and flow with him as he rises, falls, ducks and weaves.
Persevere in order to apply intrinsic energy without force,
For talent and intuition are of little use without exercise.
So be flexible, in balance and let your mind be clear and empty.

Direct your attention to the source of chi power below the navel
And with an upright body and relaxed muscles, hide your intention.
If you are pushed to the left, your foe should find no resistance.
If he then attacks to the right, pivot away like a turning wheel
Wherever your opponent strikes, he should find only emptiness
Having nothing to attack but hemmed in each time he moves away.

Be sensitive to the gentle touch in order to avoid a mighty blow.
Move forward with the stealth of a cat as it stalks a mouse
And you will learn to swoop with the skill of a hawk on a rabbit.
Let your inner stillness rest in the presence of the mountain
Overlooking the pliability of the stream descending its slopes.
In this way, your yin-yang power will work in harmony with nature.

Gathering the power of chi within is like drawing a mighty bow.
The aim and direction of your skill is like releasing an arrow.
Use your mind as a General and make chi your standard bearer.
The waist will then be your fortress to hold your inner power
And ching will arise to invigorate and purify the vital force.

KARMA
By
John Gent and Greta Dabek.

Karma is created by the action of our selfish personalities
That spread our illusions and bind us to the wheel of change.
This desire stokes the fire of passion that burns the heart
But if we conserve this power and cease to feed our craving,
We can use it for the good of others and receive our reward.

The water of the river of life always seems to be the same
But it is constantly being renewed by mountain springs above.
As we flow down the dazzling waterfalls of our inspired youth
Into the fast streams of busy, selfish and ambitious, adult life,
We then go on to enter the mighty river of old age and wisdom
But we also carry with us the poisons of our own corruption
That is purified by the salt of the mighty ocean of death.

Sun power of the Creator, recycles the water of life from the sea
In the miracle of evaporation to the cloud of unknowing rebirth
That transports us on the wind, to the mountain of conception,
To launch us in the life-germinating rain, back to Earthly form.
Once more, clean, pure and revitalised to begin another journey
Back to the ocean from the sparkling, mountain spring of childhood

This cycle of life will go on unceasing until we learn to be free
Of the wheel of change and cease to feed the passions with karma.
First we have to tame the power of personal ambition and desire
By calming the mischievous delusions of our selfish ego awareness
To free ourselves of attachment to fame, name, fortune and reward
And in contentment, lose our attachment to success and failure.

Empty yourself and let your mind rest in peace and tranquility.
Learn to be still and then the river of life will flow by
As you open your heart and mind on the bridge of illumination
And bask in innocent playfulness that is warmed by the spirit
To become one with the Creator and dwell in enlightenment.

ORDER
By
John Gent and Greta Dabek.

Order is the creative source of evolution within the universe
That turns simple elementary forces into organised complexity
Conforming to all embracing progressive and expanding rules.
This enables the invisible lifeforces to animate dormant forms
To dance to the cosmic rhythm that is played by the Creator.

The spirit that resides in the functional chemistry of the body
Works to evolve its multiplicity of forms towards perfection.
All that is good operates to this end and evil opposes it.
People do wrong through lack of knowledge and example from others
Order in external life is reflected in good conduct and love
But internally through cheerful contentment of countenance
That allows the perfection of the spirit to light up the flesh.

Jen is the essential quality of goodness expressing sympathy
And fellow feeling that creates benign order without motivation,
Self interest and thought of personal gain at others expense.
For goodness that comes directly from the human spirit and dwells
In the heart of man is infinitely better than that which emanates
From the ego and feeds personal pride with deluded superiority.

Lying and bearing false witness is the greatest sin against order
In society, that can only be prevented by complete honesty.
Truthfulness is the greatest of the five virtues of evolving life
Followed by integrity, moving impersonally without self interest
Acting for the common good that does not seek personal gain.
Only in this way, can sound judgment succeed and order prevail.

The preoccupations of the mind are mixed and forever changing
And serve only the conditioned personal world of the body.
Attention of the awareness illuminates a mirror that reflects
The immortal spirit and allows it to witness the world of change
To express its perfection through skill and compassion in life.

SELF RELIANCE
By
John Gent and Greta Dabek.

Yoga is a friend to those who learn the science of self control.
First to restrain busy thought and then to bring it to quiescence
And, by this means, the student learns to direct all his efforts.
For only those who focus the will towards calmness and composure
Can begin to break their attachment to the body and find the Self.

When we are able to curb our strong desire for material things,
We reap our reward in a detachment that leads us to inner peace.
For the cravings of the flesh multiply with their attainment
And so the appetite grows with the eating and we know no rest.
Yoga is the science of self improvement and those who follow
The path of skilful means, apply themselves totally to the task
They came here to achieve and succeed by applying Self-reliance.

Do not concern yourself with your health and future prospects
But do all you can to promote perfection in thought, word and deed
For worry and self doubt, prevent us from accepting life as it is,
Free from the sad distortions of selfish ambition and petty hate.
From this base, we can develop expertise in the art of control
By which, composure of mind and contented emotions bring us joy.

The seekers of truth are confronted everywhere by total illusion.
On one side, they find the distractions of doubt and disbelief
And on the other, they discover faith and certainty in folly.
Only the middle way of courage, patience and perseverance
Offer hope by testing practical expertise and observing results.
For those who persist in their efforts, will find peace of mind.

We are born in ignorance and darkness and search for the light
Of self satisfaction that usually results in a journey to nowhere.
Love is the switch that turns on the power of illumination
And in this compassion lies composure and contentment of spirit.
So love everyone all the time including your skeptics and enemies.

PERFECTION
By
John Gent and Greta Dabek.

Those who relax in love and practice patience and discipline
Have already begun to tread the path that leads to perfection
That forsakes the pursuit of pleasure for the illumination
Of the awareness with the light of the spirit that dwells
In the settled calm of a still mind and a loving heart.

Ignorance is the root cause of all our suffering and problems
As it mistakes the illusions of this world for the truth within.
For ego can only identify with the fortunes of the mortal body
And believes the satisfaction of its desires alone will bring pleasure
But those who follow the path of worldly ambition will suffer
Its discord, disease, old age and death, so let go this grip now
And work for freedom that reveals the perfection of the spirit.

We who liberate ourselves from the folly of conditioned life
Can only rise above it by accepting things and all that happens
With calm equilibrium that never carries the heavy burdens
Of guilt, remorse, shame and misery when reflecting on the past.
Putting our misdeeds behind us, enables us to make a fresh start
To pay for our wrongdoing and make amends by constructive action.

Let your skills develop within, through steady, untiring effort
But look not to the future for salvation. For like the past
It exists as an illusion in the mind as only the present is real.
So save your thoughts and intentions for the direct action now
To do everything as skilfully as possible and from this beginning
You will slowly improve your expertise on the road to perfection.

The student who is harmless and kind will find it in others.
Those who are always completely honest will then know the truth.
When we bring our desires under control, we will have all we need.
For those who are without craving, understand their true nature.
By single-minded, cheerful contentment, we will move to perfection.

HEALTH
By
John Gent and Greta Dabek.

Health is a voyage in calm waters and illness is a raging storm
That destroys our natural harmony of being and the rhythm of life
In which yesterday is a dream and tomorrow carries a vision
Of a bright and happy future based upon a contented present
That enables us to live with happy memory and joyful anticipation.

If we eat badly, no one can cure us but dining as nature intended
No medicine is needed as our regulating systems keep us well.
Healing takes its time and patience provides a cure when we grasp
The best way to find health is by eating little and being content.
Man alone cooks, tampers and changes the food from Nature's pantry
And suffers pain and ill health by eating for gluttonous joy.
Our search for health will end when we work in rhythm with life.

The Creator within provides everything we need and by using skill
Wisely, we make full use of our potential and abstain from folly.
For everything we eat changes our bodies for better or worse
And health is assured when we eat the best of Nature's treasure.
The greatest poison comes from eating food the body does not need
As overeating burdens it with toxins that serves to make us ill.

Total exercise of every muscle in the body is the aim of yoga.
Those who have not time for such trivialities have to make space
In life for illness that ruins pleasure and eating is a burden.
Materialists measure food in calories, proteins, fats and starches
When in reality, it is the dynamic living force that can release
The spirit and this composure and contentment cures all our ills.

Perfection of Being begins with a wholesome and balanced diet
But as our unnatural appetite devours the bounty of the Earth,
We destroy the beauty of the landscape and leave an empty desert
In its place as we contaminate our living space with corruption.
We ruin the land of our ancestors and pollute the water with trash.

THE SELF
By
John Gent and Greta Dabek.

When I become safe in the faith and power of my own immortality,
I realise the nature of the life that courses through my body
And I have trust in the strange learning process I experience.
I am at peace because what has happened in the past is over
And what is to come, will unfold in the wonder of each new day.

I feel worthwhile and the joy in my heart leaves me content
As I receive the love I long for in the warming compassion
I have for those around me as I accept the rhythm of life
And follow its perfect beat wherever it leads me in faith
That allows me to love and to be the way I am right now:
Imperfections and all. Each moment of my life is complete
As I approve of what I am and feel wanted and welcome everywhere.

I have found a new sense of wonder in the enjoyment of Being
What I am and in this state, the turmoil around me cannot break
The serenity I feel inside. This opens a door that lights reality
Before my astonished gaze and fills my whole body and senses
With a great harmony that transforms my thoughts and feelings
In a total well being that shines out from the perfection within.

I am a miniature of the universal design and that is linked
To the very essence of life itself. The power of the infinite
Is expressed through my awareness as I live each moment
In the here and now, as only the present is real and precious
And by this means alone, I will discover that which is real
That will always illude scientific method and logical complexity.

The Self is the essence of our awareness and an island of peace
That remains serene and calm during the panic and suffering
Of our daily lives. Only he remains happy in our grief and pain
And if we share his joy when our minds are filled with hatred,
We realise that he is our mortality and all that we are.

THE INNER LIGHT
By
John Gent and Greta Dabek.

We who experience the joys of yoga, have control of the mind
And as a result, become aware of the immortal unchanging Self
As the rest of us have to suffer the spiteful moods of the body.
When we are able to still our busy thoughts and unruly feelings,
We then set forth upon the lonely road that will set us free.

Experience is gained by those who have measured understanding
And this enables them to remember what is true without distortion
To overcome the entanglements of ignorance, passion and illusion.
True memory, faith, effort and concentration enable the seeker
To begin to perceive the unreality of Mayas' enchanted garden
And cease to be bound by the karma of the pairs of opposites.
We then discover that only the middle way leads to freedom.

Success results from the skills derived from intense effort
But dabblers and those that are half hearted, will lose their way.
We, who are single minded in intent and detached in our actions,
Will taste the fruits of practice and experience illumination.
For the Self is one, pure and unique and dwells in its own light
That is fed by the power of love and the delights of bliss.

Devotion is the light of the soul that knows God eternal.
His name is Om and those who keep it hallowed and sacred
Will overcome the torments of disease, doubt and distress.
So destroy hatred and fear by dwelling upon their opposites
For the mind becomes united by focusing on peace and joy.
Those who are calm, restrain the restless ego from selfishness.

Those who have the skill to quieten the mind into silence,
Can hold it still and illuminated like a lamp in a windless place
That lights our awareness with a direct understanding of truth.
They see the world as it is, without distortion or illusion
And are aware of single-minded intuition that transcends thought.

SECRETS
By
John Gent and Greta Dabek.

Secrets are understood by those who know how to control desire
But others who are held fast by lust, see only the mysteries.
Beauty and virtue exist because ugliness and evil are recognised
Along with every other pair of opposites, with each polarity
Dependent upon the other for its existence in the human world.

The way of the empty vessel links together heaven and earth
And the dualities in the biological world of flora and fauna
Which satisfies the embodied spirit without ever running dry.
It is the mother of invention by which all knots can be untied,
Every problem solved, violence calmed and tensions relaxed.
The silence that lies behind the ever-changing, mental images
And the illumination of the awareness is its journey's end.

People stay honest by ceasing to value things in short supply.
If they are unaware of what triggers desire, they will be placid.
Those who have an empty heart, a full belly and exercised sinews
Without self motivation, no longer feed off the tree of knowledge
But find sustenance in the tree of life and by actionless action
Share a wisdom they cannot own, in harmony with the invisible.

The Sage relies on actionless activity and teaches non-dual speech
That activates clear-minded attention and sees beyond near and far,
Above high and low, in-between this and that, in timeless evolution.
He achieves his aim without analysing logically what he does
And exerts benevolent control over the external, making no claim
To success from his powers and spreading the expertise to others.

Truth in humanity spreads from good government, order and faith
Through which flow the harmonious forces of universal fellowship
And leads the student of the middle way to practice gentle action
In which the detached witness remains quietly in the background
To reveal the secrets of love, freedom and life everlasting.

WONDER
By
John Gent and Greta Dabek.

Wonder grows in those who lose their exaggerated self-importance
And contemplate the vastness of space and see our insignificance.
On the universal timescale, the whole history of the human race
Is as nothing when compared to the planet on which we live
And our importance lies in our ability to observe it with wonder.

The eternal sense allows us to experience timelessness and know
The world around us with detached composure and unhurried calm.
The impatience of our restless ego, enslaves us with its haste
That takes us along the road of stress and achieves only discord
As our intense lifestyle keeps us out of harmony with nature.
By doing what we are designed to do with skill and dedication,
We can blend eternal life with its expression through the flesh.

Our sense of security becomes lost in this fearful world of pain
And constant change when nothing offers stability and permanence.
In childhood only do we feel safe even in precarious situations,
And if we choose to return to this sublime state of infancy,
We can live one day at a time and know that tomorrow will settle
The sorrows of today and we will then have the gift of grace.

The sense of simplicity is lost on those who live busy lives
In the crowded places where we share common greed and discord
And the illusory highs and lows promoted by money and power.
By taking our foot off the accelerator of our ambitious drive
And accepting life as it comes, we will steady our foolish actions
To a manageable level and follow the path to the wondrous light.

The power of harmony is lost in the stress, noise and pollution
Of busy life and this causes all our fears, ailments and pain.
Discord is the destroyer that harbours disease and shortens life.
If we can detach ourselves from the turmoil around us and rest
In the healing rhythms within, we will keep our sense of wonder.

THE GATEWAY
By
John Gent and Greta Dabek.

Illumination merges mind and body together in a state of oneness
That is me and from this source flows thought, feeling and desire
Which separates awareness from my true nature as I experience
An endless succession of impressions that creates the illusion
Of living in an enchanted world of strange forces and events.

Unless I see through the delusion presented by senses and moods
To my mind, I will become identified with the role I am designed
To play by nature and forget my true Being as I fail to learn.
For I myself create the experience I receive from the world
And know that my body is made of energy and not solid material.
I am the eternal observer who produces impressions in space-time
And when my task is done, I will realise the grand design of life.

Observing reality is a learning experience and until I am aware
That I myself am not part of the spectacle I am witnessing,
I will forever remain in the ignorance of the value of my true nature
And appear to live and die as the animals do, without purpose.
For although I appear to be separate from those who are around me
I share the same forces and patterns in my search for reality.

Time is an evolving spectacle that flows from ignorance to truth
And as I undertake this journey of becoming, eternity is lost.
For all that changes is unreal and created things pass away.
My true home is stillness and when I observe the panorama
Of life without entering the illusion, my journey is complete
And I will then realise my true nature and unite with reality.

We are one of another and although we seem to be small and weak,
It is the way our minds manufacture this illusion of the world.
For we are one with the universal life force and as we learn,
We will no longer become victims of ageing, sickness and death
As we achieve mastery of all we observe in the eternal spirit.

ILLUMINATION
By
John Gent and Greta Dabek.

The mysteries of life are not understood by reason or even faith
But by experience under the guidance of someone who is awake.
These mysteries only exist because of the limitations we impose
Because we are asleep and dream of conditioned life in the body.
In our twilight world those who are single-minded reign supreme.

Our awareness is defiled by primitive moods and motivated thought
And this can be cleansed by stillness that comes by watching.
The senses are refined by stopping action and listening intently
And when we can hear our breath and the beating of our hearts,
We will also become aware of the greater Self behind the mind
And realise that the world we see is a bad reflection of reality
That permeates our mortal frame to reveal unlimited life beyond.

Spontaneity comes when we are alert and in tune with our actions.
For well integrated people are not hemmed in by personal routine.
The analytical mind is the enemy of reality, that places barriers
To creative genius, that illuminates our awareness with truth.
Purposeful action dispels doubt and those who cannot choose,
Lose their way in a sea of confusion that clouds their judgment.

Balancing caution and recklessness is essential for perfect work
And those who develop this equanimity of mind, act with joy.
By keeping our awareness calm and contented, we stay in tune
With situations that arise and apply this harmony instantly.
When we flow in rhythm with life, then our suffering will cease
As we no longer postpone our joy of Being in the here and now.

Mood management leads to the release of harmonious hormones
That bring joy and radiate around us like a beautiful melody.
This power to banish ill will by one-pointed, undivided attention
Allows the spirit to illuminate the awareness with its presence
So that it can express its perfection in the world by our actions.

AWAKENING
By
John Gent and Greta Dabek.

The spirit is complete, whole and perfect and has no need for life
In the body and its short, pathetic existence on our tiny planet.
It is the spirit that brings life into our flesh and lights the mind
But we who have achieved yoga realisation have no need of brain
In order to think and so can understand that which is unthinkable.

Spirit, energy and matter are essential elements of the universe
As the Observer uses the instruments of observation to witness
And by this means, the Creator uses the power of creation
To build thought forms from the restless forces of yang and inert
Latent power that resides in the mysterious darkness of yin.
And yet, the spirit can see without the eye that perceives
And live eternally without the limited restrictions of the body.

The universe is manifest and unmanifest in the light and darkness.
Like two bulbs of the hour-glass with its narrow connecting
Tube, the sands of time run down from the light-filled cosmos
Of omnipresent superconsciousness into the mysterious black hole.
That is unknowable and immeasurable and land of the unconscious
Man is at the narrow neck and he can experience a little of both.

Yoga is attained as a union takes place in the awareness of man
Between the opposites of light and darkness that join yin and yang.
When we are able to awaken our awareness with the light of spirit
To explore the unmanifest darkness of the mysterious unconscious
By subliminal meditation, we realise that the time when we sleep
Is equally important as awaking life and we then achieve balance.

Total awareness can only be achieved when we cease to be attached
To our hypnotic fixation with life in the body in which primitive
Forces of flesh, hold us prisoner in confinement we cannot break.
We have no need to achieve what we already have and by the path
Of skilful means, we can awaken spirit who will set us free.

MING

By
John Gent and Greta Dabek.

Ming is the light that leads the seeker to enlightment
And brings the knowledge that leads the soul back to its origin
By an understanding of nature and the karmic wheel of change
To which all beings conform in the evolution of conditioned life.
To know ming is to understand the compassion that unites us all.

The student of ming values unity, simplicity and emptiness
Beyond any of the possessions and distractions or the world.
For emptiness within promotes undivided attention without,
Whilst the Self watches and listens in contented peace of mind.
Ten thousand things rise and fall in the world of phenomena.
They grow, flourish, pass away and are renewed again and again
In the continuous cycle of change across the eternal present.

Our aim in ming, is to return back to the source of awareness
By stilling the mind and watching the nature of external form
That changes with the seasons but remains constant in essence.
The mind that sees change but not constancy, has no roots,
But the still mind finds its inspiration in the light of spirit.
An open mind has the key which unlocks love from the heart.

A mind that is still and empty, can fill a loving heart
And forgets the scheming ego-centred, thinking machine
Out of which grew as it flowers in the light of ming.
Then the world of duality and conditioned existence melts
Like ice in the Sun that shines with limitless compassion,
And misery and frustration dissolve away and are no more.

The ming student need not fear the length of his journey
For he has all that he will ever need in this present moment
And it is he alone who is able to light up his own darkness
By uncovering the illumination confined within his own soul,
And this brings a quiet humility and love that conquers all.

THE UNIVERSE WITHIN
By
John Gent and Greta Dabek.

Merging the vital power of the body with virtue of the spirit
Unite together in the primordial egg in the mingmen cavity.
There it is fertilized with the vital seed of tai-chi from where
It moves through the portal of destiny into the tantien cauldron
For incubation from an embryo into an immortal spiritual child.

For the spiritual embryo to develop, the flesh must be pure
And the fire of the generative chi forces provide nourishment
In spiritual food by blending saliva with the breath of chi-kung.
When the body is exercised by tai-chi-chuan, the channels are open
And the yin-yang energies are blended and refined in the cavities.
The silver chord will feed the newly-formed foetus with tai-chi
Life forces ready for its journey through the mysterious gate.

Man is a universe containing three kingdoms of shen, chi and ching.
When they unite in the body between mingmen, tantien and jing gong
They surround the egg of life to give nourishment and protection
For the evolvement of the immortal child so that it may emerge
To take its place amongst the shining ones in the service of Tao.
This is a Taoist adaption of raising kundalini in Indian yoga.

The successful student travels through life empty without purpose
And he will welcome human experience and form relationships
That cross his path. Before he builds his virtue for the journey
Into the clouds, he will secure his foundations with humility
In order that he may curb the greed and sensuality of the Id.
And allow conscience and self-control to be his guiding light.

For those who fail and leave the body through the mortal gate
Life has not been in vain. For them the cycle of life goes on
And experience is valuable for those with the will to continue.
Slowly, the brutal and aggressiveness of the ape man will be tamed.
In time, wisdom and virtue will open the gates of heaven to all.

POWERS
By
John Gent and Greta Dabek.

Tao lights up the body and mind only when the ego is asleep.
When the ethereal channels open and chi flows to the tantiens
At the head, heart and navel to balance yin and yang in the body,
The powers of tai-chi and the secret of the turtle breath
Are revealed and nature shares her wisdom with the Being within.

First we allow mind and body to melt in the still waters of yin
To become soft so we can fall gently like a cushion without harm.
The yin body seals its wounds as water before the piercing sword.
But when the power of yang prevails, we become hard like steel
And the violence of nature cannot penetrate this invisible armour
As we merge ourselves with the magnetic energies of the Earth,
We become solid and immoveable in the fixed pose of a mountain.

By elevating ourselves, we can unite with the power of heaven
And become light as a feather and thereby glide upon the wind.
As we harness ourselves with the forces of radiant light,
Solar energy fills the body and we feel a merry heat in the cold,
Mountain air that protects us from the blizzard's icy blast
And we freeze away the crude, lustful sensuality of the flesh.

By cooling power of the Moon, we can walk through fire unharmed.
This leads to an even greater skill as we balance all our forces
To charm the elements of nature to be obedient to our command.
When we breathe as a little child, we will remain ever young
As our guardian chi, protects us from disease and starvation
In order that we may experience the supreme power of tai-chi.

All things become known, as the clairvoyant third eye opens
And its visions are reflected in our awareness by the mirrormind.
As we pass through life calm, unmotivated, untempted and empty
We enter the mysterious void in the shining circle of tai-chi
To find ourselves in the all-embracing Presence of the Tao.

FORCES
By
John Gent and Greta Dabek.

When we contemplate the mysterious eternal forces of the Tao
That serve all the creative manifestations of its divine will
From the tiniest atom to the mighty galaxies of the cosmos,
The primordial forms of ching merge with the intelligence of shen
To release the forces of chi that brings rhythm to the universe.

When Tao gave light to the world, tai-chi emerged from darkness
And the first polarised force was born in the form of yin and yang.
This egg of life is found in the primordial breath of yuan-chi,
Opening the door of destiny in the body at the ming-men centre.
This energy flows into the ocean of vitality below the navel
By merging the outer and inner breaths of wai-chi and nei-chi
With the yang heaven and yin earth forces together in chi-kung.

Before the circulating breath of hsing chi can complete its cycle
The practice of tai-chi-chuan is necessary to relax the meridians
And remove blockages to the flow of chi in the ethereal channels.
When this is done, the embryonic breath of tai-hsi will awaken
The embodied spirit to maintian the health and youth of the body.
Then the melting breath of lien-chi can penetrate into the system.

The breath unites the vital forces of the body through tiao-chi
As the mind is calmed and the organs are nourished by fu-chi.
This fills the middle tantien which releases its healing powers.
Then the inner breath flows in the meridians as yen-chi completes
The circuit, through the exercise of swallowing saliva, and allows
The upper tantien to illuminate the awareness with wu-chi purity.

When all the vital chi forces merge together throughout the body,
The sacred embryo Sheng-tei is energized and carries the soul
Into immortality when the flesh dissolves and the body dies.
Then the sacred infant is born again from its mortal sheath
And passes beyond the veil of death into the dimensionless void.

GAIA
By
John Gent and Greta Dabek.

The binding force of the Earth is in the gravity of its parts.
Just as water holds together the biological structure of Gaia
For the creative interaction of its rich plant and animal life,
Each holding and supporting the other in a continuous food chain
That is kept together by a single consciousness as it is in man.

Life forces bring the light of spirit into the biology of Gaia
And as the eye can catch no glimpse of it, it is called illusive.
Those who listen for it cannot hear it, call it rare and ethereal
And when we reach out and cannot find it, we label it microscopic
But field energy serves all and sustains the sense unaware of it.
Although it binds forms together, it remains formless as it leads
All intelligent creatures towards the light, it remains invisible.

Colours that please the eye and sounds that make us cry,
Smells and tastes that delight the palate, serve only the body,
But those whose touch rests within the belly, heart and mind
Can sense harmonious movement of strange unimaginable forces
That beat to a rhythm not of the body but to heavenly melody
Of the mighty Gaia as all creatures dance and respond to its tune.

The biosphere displays its wondrous creations in many forms
That move as puppets on strings of field energy and remain unknown.
So look within, you who search for life's secrets and you will find
Power in quiescence, joy in silence and Presence in stillness.
Then you will become aware of the root out of which you grew,
Linking to others, all nourished by the same power from the void.

The void beyond awareness is found by losing personal identity
And our attachment to the ebb and flow of the actions of life.
This brings immortality to those uncontaminated by word and deed
That values light before illusion and perception above thought.
The astonished wonder of the enlightened soul unites with Gaia.

REALITY
By
John Gent and Greta Dabek.

It is strange how societies down the ages build temples to gods
In the form of churches, pyramids, stone circles and shrines.
It is people who bring God to these places and no one is there.
For the body is the temple of the spirit and heaven dwells
Within it and the spirit will illuminate it if the flesh is pure.

Those who have awakened the Being within, put duty before self.
Forgiving without blaming and putting meekness before assertion.
To play the game of life well, we must remember why we are here.
This seed of God is planted in us all, neglect it and it will die
But water it with your love, nurture it with mercy and joy
And it will germinate into Being and lead us towards a light
That can pierce the darkness of ignorance and reveal the Self.

Try and be perfect slowly by eliminating errors and mending faults.
By self control and skilful means, we will learn by experience
And by forgetting what we were we will then remember who we are.
If we are able to bring the wayward and mischievous body ego
Under the direction of the spirit, we can balance the polarities.
Being good without resisting evil, we will be detached from both.

We, who seek truth, should begin by ridding ourselves of beliefs.
By the same measure, neither should we replace it with disbelief.
For only by becoming precariously generalised can we comprehend
The magnitude of the reality that surrounds us, and the vast
Minature world within the confines of our bodies, and realise
There are worlds within worlds all operating to the same plan.

If we begin to understand the reality we live with each day
As it unfolds before us in the moving moment in time, we will find
Far greater results than we can by studying the ideas of others.
So keep your faith steady in the knowledge that truth is found
In Self, not in fresh experience, but in remembering who you are.

TAO
By
John Gent and Greta Dabek.

The inferior man works through his feelings and physical power.
The evolved student acts with measured restraint and discernment.
The brute charges into the hedge like a goat and gets entangled.
We who wish to unite with Tao do not walk the paths of the masses
And follow the lonely way of the clouds in the mysterious void.

When we have travelled far, then it is time to stop and reflect
And wait patiently for the best opportunity for further advance.
By adjusting our action to rest in harmony with the forces
Of yin and yang, our movements follow the cycles of nature
And never miss an opportunity through laziness of distraction.
Then we can withdraw before the raging elements without harm
And by restraining our anger and impatience, conserve our power.

Punishing the folly of others does not allow us to be foolish.
Chance is a fickle mistress likely to bestow favour on our foes
But in the long run, perseverance is likely to bring good fortune,
So we should feel no bitterness and remorse over lost opportunity
But gather our forces and preserve them for the next happy day
When we can use them to serve the aimless, non-acting will of Tao.

Rest happily in what you have as the joy you now experience
Is worth more than riches bought in the coin of avarice and greed.
For this carefree abandonment you now feel is the real success.
These spiritual energies cannot be grasped but are very strong.
In the same way that water patiently wears away the hardest rock
So the flexible man avoids obstacles and becomes rigid in death.

The student of Tao, moves with gentleness and harmony and unfolds
His actions like a flower in the Sun and closes before the damp.
Superior man relies not on himself but on application to task.
He will fight without anger and defend himself without intent
And when the day is done will rest peacefully in the empty Tao.

CHI-KUNG

By

John Gent and Greta Dabek.

We enter this world through the mortal door
To find our way to the mysterious gate.
Our purpose is to slay dragons and tame tigers
With the sword of metal and lance of wood
And so we learn to ride the wind with the crane.

Those who climb the mountain of immortality
Find their reward in the secret beyond the clouds.
As we scale the tsu-wang meditation to emptiness
We find that both heaven and earth dwell within us
And when we harmonise them together in perfect balance
We discover the hidden mysteries of the inner Being
And experience sung in the primordial breath of Tao.

The secret breath of chi-kung refines our inner power
With the serene emptiness of wu and purity of shen
And we feel light as a feather to ride the clouds
As we free ourselves from personal motivations
And in a quiet state of humility, forget who we are
In the delight of helping others along the way.

First we must mix the yang energies of heaven
With the cooling yin forces of the earth
So that our inner tiger can work with the dragon
In balanced harmony to fly with the crane
Into the gentle clouds of sung and become aware
Of tai-chi and find the wisdom of the masters.

We come here into this world of joy and sadness
Through the mortal gate of ignorant illusion
And will remain in this animal state until we refine
Our vital forces with the purifying breath of chi-kung
And thereby discover our true nature beyond the veil.

THE SAGE
By
John Gent and Greta Dabek.

The Shen Jen Sage has no axe to grind and no ambitions to realise.
He has no gods to appease and no time for trivial loves and hates.
He follows the way to Tao and is dependent on nothing and no one.
By remaining calm and steadfast in an uncertain, changing world,
He captures the essence of nature by penetrating appearances.

His resolve holds firm by patience, perseverance and persistence.
As he observes no system of rules and policies made to be broken,
Instead, he follows the natural law that evolves through his body
As he knows that false boundaries create nothing but conflict.
And by being harmless and self-sustaining, he will observe reality
Behind the illusory opposites of love and hate, life and death,
By remaining composed, contented and balanced, he follows the way.

The art of getting things skilfully done achieves more and more
By less effort and he that does nothing, learns to ride upon
The natural forces with the grace of a great, hovering bird.
The spirit in man does nothing but by its presence and command
All things are done as great works arise out of humble genius
And gentle release of purposeful energy has powerful effect.

When the mind goes beyond thought into controlling field energy,
The awareness moves from passion to peace and activity to repose.
For those who have faith will know how to work without the ego,
Knowledge is a functional understanding that hides the very truth
It expressed as its rain of detail drenches the creative fire.
Reasoning builds smug cleverness and pride that denies wisdom.

Non-action does not imply laziness but flows in rhythm with nature
And by not interfering in the order of things, harmony prevails.
We travel across mountains and rivers in our vain quest for Tao
Without realising that he has been our companion all the way.
Difficulty rises from disharmony and suffering disappears in love.

ENLIGHTENMENT
By
John Gent and Greta Dabek.

Mindful awakefulness holds our attention upon the target of life
And when our aim is true and our skill is based on experience
We will not fall short or overshoot our mark and in this way
Can forget desire, embrace simplicity and humbly follow the path
And know that we are the immortal observer of the drama of life.

Success turns to ruin if we then believe that we are special
But failure can bring a better reward in humility and patience
As improvement begins when we no longer need to impress others.
The tree of knowledge withers as memory fades but experience
Awakens conscience and allows the tree of life to flourish
In spirit who knows that the seed that grows towards eternity
Is greater than the universe revolving around its tiny centre.

The practicalities of life are complex and a state of many laws
Also has the most law breakers as legislation produces outlaws.
However, the child that steals a penny will one day rob a bank
And punishment only incites rebellion and mischief in the young.
And now the old and wise are no longer valued in our society
They fail to tell us that laws are obeyed because they protect us.

Virtue is wisdom in action and error is folly expressing delusion
But only the wise refuse to become entangled in lustful pleasure
And welcome suffering as the best way to learn from our mistakes.
For those who pass beyond the limitations of belief and doubt
Will know the secret of karma and its law of cause and effect
That shapes our lives in opposites that bind us to the wheel.

The spirit observes without function but is lost in attachment
And although immortal, is unaware of this and as a result suffers
With the body and identifies with the drama and spectacle of life.
Only when it begins to see through the illusion can it be free
To realise its own immortality and so choose to be enlightened.

THE WITNESS
By
John Gent and Greta Dabek.

Illumination is a merging together of mind and body in a oneness
That is me and from this source flow thought, feeling and desire,
That separates my awareness from my true nature and I experience
The endless succession of impressions that creates the illusion
Of living in an enchanted world of strange events and forces.

Unless I see through the delusions of my senses and thoughts
That fill my mind, I am identified with the role I am designed
By nature to play, and forget my true nature as I fail to learn.
For it is I that create the experience I receive from this world
And my body is composed of intelligent energy and not material.
I am the eternal Witness that creates impressions upon time
And when my task is done, I will realise the grand plan of life.

Observing reality is a learning experience and until I am aware
That I myself am not a part of the spectacle I am witnessing
I will forever remain in ignorance and not know my true nature
And appear to live and die as animals, without aim or purpose.
For although I seem to be separate and independent from others,
I share the same forces and life pattern in my search for reality.

Time is an evolving spectacle that flows from ignorance to truth
And as I make this journey on the river of life, eternity is lost.
For all that changes is unreal and created things will pass away.
My true home is stillness and when I observe the moving panorama
Of life without entering into the illusion, my journey is complete
And I will realise my true nature in perfect oneness with reality.

We are one of another and although we may appear small and weak
This is only how our minds perceive the world and its illusions.
For we alone are one with the universal life-force and as we know this,
We will no linger become victims of ageing, sickness and death
And achieve mastery of all we observe in eternal spiritual Being.

THE INNER WILL
By
John Gent and Greta Dabek.

The human body is weak and fragile and can be broken like a jar
But when filled with the power of mind illuminated by spirit
It becomes a fortress to withstand the onslaught of living.
Its walls bristle with the weapons of knowledge and the arsenal
Of experience that is devoted to conquering the deluded ego.

Angry thoughts promote spiteful action and desire for revenge
Upon those on whom we vent our wrath and as our discord grows,
Pain and misery follow us with the certainty of our own shadow.
If instead we treat adversaries as our friends and love them
In spite of what they do, we will retain our inner harmony to heal
The terror and torment they impose on us and get on with life
To fulfill the task we came for to escape the bondage of illusion.

Truth will not find a home with those whose thoughts are selfish
And those who live in arrogance and greed will never know reality.
As rain soaks into a badly neglected house to spoil its contents
So will passions penetrate a disorderly mind and promote discord,
As we morn past follies and brace ourselves for terrors to come.
By remaining awake among the sleeping masses, we will find light.

When we arise from our sleep and observe the wonders around us,
We will realise the part we are designed to play in the world.
By directing our attention towards simplicity, our minds
Become illuminated as we attune ourselves to the inner will
That lies beyond the flesh and the limitations of our bodies,
And as experience brings success it encourages others to follow.

Thought directed by the inner will is carried upon the breath
To its target by skilful means and this tool will unveil reality
Before our astonished gaze as life in the flesh fades away
And we flow in rhythm with the greater life beyond its senses.
In this altered state, the Self finds perfection in eternity.

SUNG
By
John Gent and Greta Dabek.

When we are free of fixed rigidity, we have sung in our posture
As stiff strength and brute force disappear from our movements.
Then we know when to yield and the right time to move forward,
As our turbulent emotions disappear before the quiet command
Of sung that holds our forces poised in balance for every action.

When I feel the power of sung I rest my body in silent stillness
In order that the spirit within can take over my awareness
Without hindrance in order to fill my mind with wisdom and love.
This enables me to forget the mundane boredom of daily life
And allows me to experience the true wonder and grandeur
Of our planetary home and I can then make a small contribution
Towards the grand design of the intelligence that created it.

When I cease to shut out the spirit from my emotional nature,
I no longer have anger and hatred towards those who provoke me
And I feel a new form of love energy that radiates from my heart.
This wonderful mood of compassion fills every atom of my body
With the most delightful benevolence that travels outwards
Through my actions to infect those around me with the joy I feel.

Sung empties the mind of despair and frustration and brings joy
From the inner Being, who restores our confidence and peace,
So that we can commune with Tao at the level of purest love.
When the power of sung flows unhindered through our bodies,
We can discover the bliss of being human and raise our respect
For the genius of the Creator who made all this to open our eyes.

Sung frees our minds from evil intent so we are free to be kind.
This enables us to give and forgive others in equal measure
And we have morality without piety through gentle tolerance,
So we no longer treasure our possessions and are free from worry.
As we liberate ourselves from pride and heal ourselves with sung.

Printed in the United States
By Bookmasters